Table of Contents

PREFACE

The study and practice of magick (an an alternative spelling of magic that emphasizes magick as a more studied/scholarly enterprise and practice) can easily become one of your most fulfilling and wonderful experiences! With a fuller understanding of both the traditional and occult nature of things, you'll find yourself capable of having a significant impact on your environment.

Next to increase your skill and further your appreciation of how a multitude of outside factors can affect the outcome of your spells, I recommend you devote serious effect to mindfully journaling and accurately logging your spell casting. If this interests you, check out **Moon Magic Log Tracker | A Guided Journal for Spell-casters.**

Enjoy!

DISPLAY OF COMMON INVOCATION STANCES AND POSES

Below are illustrations of common poses assumed during
ceremonial magick. Use these as reference points and adjust
as necessary to adopt the form that best suits you. You may
assume multiple stances during your spell work, and should
allow your intuition to guide your movements.

PERFORMING THE MAGICK CIRCLE CONSECRATION SPELL

1. Draw a circle on the floor around your alter for protection against hostile forces. Be certain to make it large enough for you to assume your invocation pose(s) without allowing your extended arms, legs, or body to extend beyond the confines of your circle.

2. Approximately 3, 6, or 9 ft from your protection circle, draw apart another for the deity/spirit summoned approximately 3 feet in diameter.

3. Light a black candle on your alter, and say the Spell for Centering.

4. Dress in all black and drape yourself with a black cloth or wear a black, hooded robe.

5. Light sticks of incense: myrrh, frankincense, and sandalwood.

6. Assume your chosen invocation pose.

7. Holding the incense sticks, say the Magic Circle Consecration spell.

8. Say your chosen spell.

9. State your intention(s)/desire(s) – no more than three. You may also write them on paper and burn them using the flame from the black candle.

10. Release the spell binding the entity.

11. Light a stick of sage incense or smudge stick. Say a spell for protection.

12. Carefully stick your foot outside of circle. If you have ANY sense of foreboding or negative energy, do not attempt to leave the circle! Let the incense burn for

approximately 5 minutes, and then try again. If the hostile energy remains, summon the entity again to request assistance in expelling the hostile force(s).

13. Turn on a fan, open a window or door(s) and walk slowly throughout the space with the sage incense/smudge stick until it the energy feels properly balanced.

A SPELL FOR CENTERING

O [Entity/Spirit],
To the darkest mysteries and ways you hold the key.
Unleash your power unto me!
Spring open my heart and mind's gate!
I invoke the power to influence this my fate
With all the strength of my will.
Let the threads of fate be stilled.
Now, banish all other thought.
My will focus firmly on what is now sought:
[State your desire.]
I impel you, [Entity], to grant this to me.
As I will; so, let it be! (3x)

THE MAGICK CIRCLE CONSECRATION SPELL

O [Entity/Spirit],

To the darkest mysteries and ways you hold the key.

Unleash your power unto me!

Ascending with the power of both the dark and the light,

I pray you direct me to what is right.

Against hostile forces now set a ward –

Let this magick circle be my guard

O [Entity]!

See my sacrifice.

Hear my plea.

Come and reveal thyself to me!

Grant the request I bring now to thee.

[State your desire.]

A SPELL FOR OPENING THE SUMMONING CIRCLE

O [Entity/Spirit],

To the darkest mysteries and ways you hold the key.

Unleash your power unto me!

Pour thy secrets and ways in me beyond the brim.

My hesitation and enemies throttle and stem.

I beseech you power through this book's lines.

[State your desire.]

Reveal what's needed for us to bind,

And I'll bind us forever so tight.

I beseech you with the powers of light.

I impel you, [Entity], come now to me.

As I will, let it be! (3x)

A SPELL FOR SACRIFICE

O [Entity/Spirit],
To the darkest mysteries and ways you hold the key.
Unleash your power unto me!
For thy aid in this sacred space,
I offer thee this sacrifice in this place.
My heart, mind, and possessions I did scour
For sacrifice in exchange for your power.
I invoke the powers of three,
Bow my head, and bend the knee.
I offer this and myself to thee.
[State your desire.]
I impel you, [Entity], to grant this to me.
As I will; so, let it be! (3x)

AN INVOCATION TO A BINDING UNION

O [Entity/Spirit],

To the darkest mysteries and ways you hold the key.

Unleash your power unto me!

I beseech you to take me as you vessel.

Bring me close, my being please nestle.

Your awesome power makes me gasp.

Seize me now with your fearsome grasp.

I request an awe-inspiring wisdom,

And the resources to build my own earthly kingdom.

[State your desire.]

Grant your power unto me.

As I will; so, let it be! (3x)

A SPELL FOR A PHYSICAL MANIFESTATION

O [Entity/Spirit],

To the darkest mysteries and ways you hold the key.

Unleash your power unto me!

Come to me now in your pure and mystical form,

For I invoke thee now against hardship's storm

Use thy power both light and dark

to place me on destiny's most favored arc.

[State your desire.]

Reveal to me the cost of what I ask.

What must I do to make my fortunes last?

I impel you, [Entity], to grant this to me.

As I will, let it be! (3x)

A SPELL FOR BINDING

O [Entity/Spirit],

To the darkest mysteries and ways you hold the key.

Unleash your power unto me!

Before our union, I was bruised and tossed by

fate's vicious storms and bitting winds.

My sole yearning was for the pain to end.

With your intervention, may I continue

to know certainty and peace.

Grant me such and I sacrifices and service will not cease.

O [Entity], let thy mysterious power be mine!

In this magick ceremony, I do us bind.

[State your desire.]

I impel you, [Entity], to grant this to me.

As I will, let it be! (3x)

A SPELL FOR POWER

O [Entity/Spirit],
To the darkest mysteries and ways you hold the key.
Unleash your power unto me!
I pray that you cleanse my soul
While in the pursuit of the power to make myself whole
I seek a satisfaction so deep and profound
A desire to which I'm utterly bound
I invoke your powerful, immortal force
To put me on success' inexorable course
[State your desire.]
I impel you, [Entity], to grant this to me.
As I will; so, let it be! (3x)

A PLEDGE OF SERVICE

O [Entity/Spirit],

To the darkest mysteries and ways you hold the key.

Unleash your power unto me!

I'm prepared to do whatever you do deign.

I love you dearly and would be loved fain.

Forever bound, we are of one mind.

And willingly so! I'm glad to be thine.

There is no questioning my devotion to thee:

You've consumed my essence entirely.

[State your desire.]

I impel you, [Entity], to bestow your favor on me.

As I will, let it be! (3x)

A PLEDGE OF SUBMISSION

O [Entity/Spirit],

To the darkest mysteries and ways you hold the key.

Unleash your power unto me!

Our covenant remains ever on my mind.

My essence and you forever entwined.

Dedicated and ascendant, I'm ready for

whatever next is in store.

I've seen and felt your power & pray that you share more.

Thank you for such wondrous pleasures you've granted to me!

Guide me to wherever I need to be.

[State your desire.]

I impel you, [Entity], to grant this to me.

As I will; so, let it be! (3x)

AN INVOCATION FOR GUIDANCE AND PROTECTION

O [Entity/Spirit],

To the darkest mysteries and ways you hold the key.

Unleash your power unto me!

Swallow me in your protective shroud

And grant me all things that's allowed

For in your power, I have no doubt

I invoke your power and amazing things come about.

Guide me true, and guide me far

I yearn to be wherever you are!

[State your desire.]

I impel you, [Entity], to grant this to me.

As I will; so, let it be! (3x)

A PLEA FOR SAFETY

O [Entity/Spirit],

To the darkest mysteries and ways you hold the key.

Unleash your power unto me!

Deem not my sacrifices false nor less

I stand before you in the utmost humbleness.

In your armor I pray thyself shod.

Cleanse my soul most beautiful God,

In the midst of these spells,

Grasp my soul and secure it in your unbreakable snare.

[State your desire.]

I impel you, [Entity], to grant this to me.

As I will; so, let it be! (3x)

AN INVOCATION FOR AN INSTRUCTION

O [Entity/Spirit],

To the darkest mysteries and ways you hold the key.

Unleash your power unto me!

Teach me thy ways, doctrine, and ancient truths;

I properly submit my appeals to you:

As my immense desire aches and grows;

So you improve my position by your throes!

I praise you to skies above.

Make me worthy of your attention, favor, and your love!

[State your desire.]

I impel you, [deity], to grant this to me.

As I will, let it be! (3x)

A PLEA FOR GUIDANCE

O [Entity/Spirit],
To the darkest mysteries and ways you hold the key.
Unleash your power unto me!
[State your desire.]
Now reveal to me the cost of this intention's toll,
and how to properly perform my role.
I impel you, [Entity], to grant this to me.
As I will; so, let it be! (3x)

A SPELL FOR SUCCESS & ACCEPTANCE OF CONSEQUENCES

O [Entity/Spirit],

To the darkest mysteries and ways you hold the key.

Unleash your power unto me!

I beseech thee for an impressive domain:

Establish a kingdom in my name,

Steel me now for consequences of this campaign,

Through all hardship, my being sustain.

Your humble servant I shall remain.

I will be strong and now soberly acquiesce

To whatever sacrifices are necessary for my success

[State your desire.]

I impel you, [Entity], to grant this to me.

As I will; so, let it be! (3x)

A SPELL FOR SUCCESS, HEALTH, AND WEALTH

O [Entity/Spirit],
To the darkest mysteries and ways you hold the key.
Unleash your power unto me!
Look favorably on all I bring to this mystic fire –
All the things for which I truly desire
Coalesce, fulfill, strengthen the roots of all my things,
Grant me a well from which success, health, and wealth
spring.
I ache for this deeply – down to my very bones,
a majestic fate of my own.
[State your desire.]
I impel you, [Entity], to grant this to me.
As I will; so, let it be! (3x)

A SPELL FOR CHARISMA

O [Entity/Spirit],
To the darkest mysteries and ways you the key.
Unleash your power unto me!
I ask lips of honey and quickness of thought
To utilize fully the things our magick hath wrought.
I know, and know thee full well,
Now, I invoke your power for this spell,
[State your desire.]
I impel you, [Entity], to grant this to me.
As I will; so, let it be! (3x)

A SPELL FOR STRENGTH

O [Entity/Spirit],

To the darkest mysteries and ways you hold the key.

Unleash your power unto me!

I invoke the strength to handle whatever I come upon.

Dispel all my troubles and lead me on.

I embrace my future and wisdom from my past.

Take me to you now and hold me fast.

[State your desire.]

I impel you, [Entity], to grant this to me.

As I will; so, let it be! (3x)

A SPELL FOR TERRIFYING FIERCENESS

O [Entity/Spirit],
To the darkest mysteries and ways you the key.
Unleash your power unto me!
Not a mere semblance, but in thyself true power
Fill me with it now and make it flower
All we have willed, hoped or dreamed shall exist;
Grant me signs so that I may steadily persist
For unto you am I bound
and so unyielding, utterly terrifying on my battlegrounds
Let my adversaries cries fill the sky
So powerful soon shall be I.
[State your desire.]
I impel you, [Entity], to grant this to me.
As I will; so, let it be! (3x)

A SPELL FOR TRIUMPH OVER ONE'S ADVERSARIES

O [Entity/Spirit],

To the darkest mysteries and ways you hold the key.

Unleash your power unto me!

My spirit soars, my enemies lurk.

Let them be bound tightly, and not affect my work.

O [Entity], hear my heartfelt praise!

Come to me now and instruct me in your ways.

For my ultimate triumph, mold me to your design.

Grant me this thing I desire to make mine:

[State your desire.]

I impel you, [Entity], to grant this to me.

As I will; so, let it be! (3x)

A SPELL FOR RAPTURE

O [Entity/Spirit],

To the darkest mysteries and ways you hold the key.

Unleash your power unto me!

Take me to you for I
So that I may sit contently on high
I conquer and I rend
The depths I'm willing to reach, few can comprehend
Make my enemies quiver and shake
As everything from them I take.
Grant me power and endless majesty,
To my weakness and failings I pray you rend,

I increase my power to accept and comprehend:

[State your desire.]

I impel you, [Entity], to grant this to me.

As I will; so, let it be! (3x)

A POWERFUL REMINDER OF FAITHFUL SERVICE

O [Entity/Spirit],

To the darkest mysteries and ways you hold the key.

Unleash your power unto me!

Strengthen and propel me through fears

Never I dithered nor never agonized

Over the sacrifices deemed necessary for my prize.

My lust, my grace, my dreams, and my fears –

I'll relinquish much of what I previously held dear

Raise me up, free from others' schemes and woes.

Steady my rise through these ebbs and flows.

[State your desire.]

I impel you, [Entity], to grant this to me.

As I will; so, let it be! (3x)

A REQUEST FOR BLESSINGS

O [Entity/Spirit],

To the darkest mysteries and ways you hold the key.

Unleash your power unto me!

By the light of this magick flame,

I now invoke your ineffable name!

Builder and maker of fortunes with your sacred hands.

Wishing I can feel your power steadily expand.

[State your desire.]

I impel you, [Entity], to grant this to me.

As I will; so, let it be! (3x)

A REFLECTION AND A REQUEST

O [Entity/Spirit],

To the darkest mysteries and ways you hold the key.

Unleash your power unto me!

Consecrated now, and sacrificed whole;

So, did I promise my very soul.

What was the true cost of its worth?

And what did it unleash upon this vicious earth?

Did I give enough thought – take an adequate pause?

Did I fully consider the consequences it'd cause?

Enough! I considered when I pledged myself to thee,

Now [insert name of deity], grant what you promised me.

[State your desire.]

As I will, let it be! (3x)

RELEASING THE DEITY/SPIRIT

O [Entity/Spirit],
To the darkest mysteries and ways you the key.
Unleash your power unto me!
I give you my thanks, and release you gratefully back.
May this binding between us grow slack.
Your power and wisdom, I do pray to keep near,
And hope my future calls you here.
My guide and my might, I bid you farewell;
So, I release you gratefully with this spell.